A CourseGuide for

Greek for the Rest of Us

William Mounce

ZONDERVAN ACADEMIC

A CourseGuide for Greek for the Rest of Us

Copyright © 2019 by William Mounce

Requests for information should be addressed to:
Zondervan, *3900 Sparks Dr. SE, Grand Rapids, Michigan 49546*

ISBN 978-0-310-11114-6 (softcover)

All Scripture quotations, unless otherwise indicated, are taken from The Holy Bible, New International Version®, NIV®. Copyright © 1973, 1978, 1984, 2011 by Biblica, Inc.® Used by permission of Zondervan. All rights reserved worldwide. www.Zondervan.com. The "NIV" and "New International Version" are trademarks registered in the United States Patent and Trademark Office by Biblica, Inc.®

Any internet addresses (websites, blogs, etc.) and telephone numbers in this book are offered as a resource. They are not intended in any way to be or imply an endorsement by Zondervan, nor does Zondervan vouch for the content of these sites and numbers for the life of this book.

No part of this publication may be reproduced, stored in a retrieval system, or transmitted in any form or by any means — electronic, mechanical, photocopy, recording, or any other — except for brief quotations in printed reviews, without the prior permission of the publisher.

Agent line goes here if needed.

Printed in the United States of America

CONTENTS

Introduction 5

1. The Greek Language..................................... 7
2. The Greek Alphabet 10
3. The Greek Pronunciation 13
4. English Grammar: Noun Inflection...................... 16
5. Greek Grammar: Nouns 19
6. Prepositions 22
7. English Grammar: Verb Inflection 25
8. Greek Grammar: Verbs (Indicative) 28
9. Greek Grammar: Verbs (Nonindicative) 31
10. Word Studies 34
11. Cases 37
12. Pronouns 40
13. Modifiers 44
15. Verbal Aspect 48
16. Verbs (Voice)... 51
17. Verbs (Tense) 54
18. Verbs (Nonindicative) 57

19. **Participles** 60

20. **Conjunctions** 63

22. **Pronouns** 65

23. **Definite Article, and Odds 'n Ends** 68

24. **Adjectives** 71

25. **Phrases and Clauses** 74

27. **Nouns** 77

28. **Verbs (Indicative)** 80

29. **Verbs (Nonindicative)** 83

31. **The History of the Bible and Textual Criticism** 86

32. **Translations** 89

33. **How to Read a Commentary** 92

Introduction

Welcome to *A CourseGuide for Greek for the Rest of Us*. These guides were created for formal and informal students alike who want to engage deeper in biblical, theological, or ministry studies. We hope this guide will provide an opportunity for you to grow not only in your understanding but also in your faith.

How to Use This Guide

This guide is meant to be used in conjunction with the book *Greek for the Rest of Us* and its corresponding videos, *Greek for the Rest of Us Video Lectures*. After you have read each chapter in the book and watched the accompanying video lesson, the materials in this guide will help you review and assess what you have learned. Application-oriented questions are included as well.

Each CourseGuide has been individually designed to best equip you in your studies, but in general you can expect the following components. Most CourseGuides begin every chapter with a "You Should Know" section, which highlights key terminology, people, and facts to remember. This section serves as a helpful summary for directing your studies. Reflection questions, typically two to three per chapter, prompt you to summarize key points you've learned. Discussion questions invite you to an even deeper level of engagement. Finally, most chapters will end with a short quiz to test your retention. You can find the answer key to each quiz at the bottom of the page following it.

For Further Study

CourseGuides accompany books and videos from some of the world's top biblical and theological scholars. They may be used independently or in small groups or classrooms, offering quality instruction to equip students for academic and ministry pursuits. If you would like to engage in further study with Zondervan's CourseGuides, the full lineup may be viewed online. After completing your studies with *A CourseGuide for Greek for the Rest of Us*, we recommend moving on to *A CourseGuide for Basics of Biblical Greek*, and *A CourseGuide for Four Portraits, One Jesus*.

CHAPTER 1

The Greek Language

You Should Know

- Linear B: the earliest form of the Greek language
- Classical Greek: the form of Greek used by writers from Homer through Plato
- Phoenician: the basis of the Greek alphabet
- Attic Greek: a prominent and developed dialect of Greek spoken by Alexander the Great
- Aristotle: the Greek philosopher who tutored Alexander the Great
- Koine: the common, everyday form of the Greek language used by everyday people
- The Septuagint: the Greek translation of the Old Testament used by Hellenized Jews at the time of Christ
- Proto-Indo-European: a group of language families that includes Romance, Germanic, Old Greek, and Aryan languages
- English: a Germanic language that integrates words from Greek, Latin, and French
- Semitic languages: languages such as Hebrew and Aramaic that are not Indo-European

Essay Questions

1. What does it mean that Koine was the language of the common people?

2. How is Greek a part of the English language? What kinds of words did we adopt from it?

Quiz

1. (T/F) The earliest form of the Greek language is called "Linear C."

2. (T/F) The form of Greek used by writers from Homer through Plato is called Classical Greek.

3. (T/F) The Greek alphabet was derived from the Phoenicians.

4. (T/F) The three primary Greek dialects were Doric, Aeolic, and Attic.

5. (T/F) Alexander the Great was tutored by the Greek philosopher Plato.

6. Alexander the Great spoke:
   a) Attic Greek
   b) Koine Greek
   c) Doric Greek
   d) Classical Greek

7. Which of the following means "common" and was the common, everyday form of the Greek language used by everyday people?
   a) Attic Greek
   b) Koine Greek
   c) Doric Greek
   d) Classical Greek

8. Which type of Greek is used in the Septuagint, the New Testament, and the writings of the apostolic fathers?
   a) Attic Greek
   b) Koine Greek
   c) Doric Greek
   d) Classical Greek

9. Which of the following is NOT of the Proto-Indo-European language family?
   a) Italian
   b) Dutch
   c) Aramaic
   d) Sanskrit

10. English is a Germanic language that integrated words from:
    a) Greek
    b) Latin
    c) French
    d) All of the above

ANSWER KEY
1. F, 2. T, 3. T, 4. F, 5. F, 6. a, 7. b, 8. b, 9. c, 10. d

CHAPTER 2

The Greek Alphabet

You Should Know

- Transliteration: the equivalent of a word in another language's alphabet

- Sigma: the letter for the sound "s," which has two forms, ς for the end of a word and σ elsewhere

- The consonants that create a nasal when paired with gamma: γ, κ, χ, ξ

- The Greek vowels: α (alpha), ε (epsilon), η (ēta), ι (iōta), ο (omicron), υ (upsilon), ω (ōmega)

- Iota subscript: an improper diphthong that does not affect pronunciation but does affect meaning

- Upsilon: The transliteration of υ is "*u*" if it is preceded by a vowel and "*y*" if it occurs as a single vowel.

- Capital: a script made up of mostly straight lines, often carved into rock in ancient times. In Greek texts today it is used at the beginning of proper names, quotations, and paragraphs.

- Uncial: a script with more curves, used on papyrus and parchment

- Miniscule: the smaller, cursive script, which was faster to write and conserved parchment

- Modern Greek pronunciation: a more beautiful and flowing pronunciation than the Erasmian pronunciation used in this book

Essay Questions

1. Copy a Greek verse from the New Testament or this unit's text and then transliterate it into English letters. Transliterate your normal English paragraph from above into Greek characters (with accents).

2. We currently have 2,867 New Testament miniscule manuscripts (eighth or ninth century). What does this mean for our textual certainty of the New Testament?

Quiz

1. (T/F) Modern Greek uses a different and more beautiful pronunciation scheme.

2. (T/F) Greek has 6 vowels (α, ε, η, ι, ο, υ).

3. (T/F) Sigma is written ς when it occurs at the end of the word and σ elsewhere.

4. (T/F) A translation is the equivalent of a letter in another language.

5. (T/F) Originally Greek was written in all capital letters with no spaces or punctuation.

6. Which of the following is the closest English equivalent to η?

   a) n
   b) e
   c) Both
   d) None of the above

7. Which of the following is the closest English equivalent to ω?

   a) o
   b) w
   c) Both
   d) None of the above

8. Which of the following is the closest English equivalent to υ?

   a) u
   b) y

c) Both
   d) None of the above

9. Which of the following is the closest English equivalent to χ?
   a) x
   b) k
   c) Both of the above
   d) None of the above

10. Which of the following is the closest English equivalent to ι?
    a) i as in hit
    b) ee as in seed
    c) Both of the above
    d) None of the above

ANSWER KEY

1. T, 2. F, 3. T, 4. F, 5. T, 6. b, 7. a, 8. c, 9. d, 10. c

CHAPTER 3

The Greek Pronunciation

You Should Know

- The Greek diphthongs with their pronunciation:
    - αι: aisle (Erasmian); met (Modern)
    - αυ: outhouse (Erasmian); cadaver (Modern)
    - ει: veil (Erasmian); spit, petite (Modern)
    - ευ, ηυ: eulogy (Erasmian); evangel (Modern)
    - οι: oil (Erasmian); spit, petite (Modern)
    - ου: root (Erasmian and Modern)
    - υι: quit, whisker (Erasmian); spit, petite (Modern)

- The combinations of Greek vowels that are not diphthongs and are pronounced separately: εα, εε, οο

- Greek question mark: a semicolon (;)

- Greek semicolon: a period above the line (·)

- Greek rough breathing mark: ὁ

- Greek acute accent: ά

- Greek circumflex: ῶ

- Greek grave accent: ὸ

- Greek smooth breathing mark: ἀ

- Iota subscript: ῳ

Essay Questions

1. Copy a Greek verse from the New Testament or this unit's text and then try reading it with the rising, falling, and fluttering pitch accents.

2. Copy a Greek verse from the New Testament or this unit's text and put spaces between the syllables, grouping consonants and vowels according to pronunciation.

Quiz

1. (T/F) A diphthong is a combination of two vowels that produce one sound.

2. (T/F) Almost every Greek word has an accent mark.

3. (T/F) A single consonant goes with the preceding vowel, as in αὐτ-ός (not αὐ-τός).

4. (T/F) A consonant cluster that forms a single sound goes with the following vowel.

5. (T/F) Originally the accent was a pitch accent, but now it signifies stress.

6. What does the Greek punctuation ; mean in English?
   a) ,
   b) .
   c) ;
   d) ?

7. What does the Greek punctuation . mean in English?
   a) ,
   b) .
   c) ;
   d) ?

8. The second vowel in a Greek diphthong is never:
   a) ι
   b) υ

c) η
d) ο

9. What does the accent in Ἰησοῦς signify?

    a) Rising
    b) Falling
    c) Rising and falling
    d) None of the above

10. Which of the following is NOT a Greek breathing mark?

    a) ἡ
    b) ἀ
    c) ή
    d) None of the above

ANSWER KEY

1. T, 2. T, 3. F, 4. T, 5. T, 6. d, 7. b, 8. c, 9. c, 10. c

CHAPTER 4

English Grammar: Noun Inflection

You Should Know

- Inflection: when the form of a word changes because it performs different functions in a sentence or it changes its meaning

- Noun: a word that stands for someone or something (i.e., a person, place, or thing)

- Pronoun: a word that stands in place of a noun

- Word order: how English determines which nouns perform the action of the verb, which nouns received the action of the verb, etc.

- Case: tells what relation the noun has to the verb or other nouns

- Subjective case: when a word is the subject of a verb

- Possessive case: when a word shows possession

- Objective case: when a word is the direct object

- Number: indicates whether a noun is singular or plural

- Natural gender: when words (mostly pronouns) inflect based upon whether they are referring to a masculine, feminine, or neuter object

Essay Questions

1. What is the difference between an indirect and direct object?

2. What are some common characteristics of masculine nouns? Of feminine nouns? Of neuter nouns?

Quiz

1. (T/F) Inflection is when the form of a word changes because it performs different functions in a sentence or it changes its meaning.

2. (T/F) The third person pronoun is one of the most inflected words in English.

3. (T/F) A noun is a word that stands for someone or something.

4. (T/F) Most English words change to indicate gender.

5. (T/F) English uses the order of words to determine which word is doing the action of the verb, receiving the action, etc.

6. Which of the following stands for someone or something?
    a) Noun
    b) Pronoun
    c) Both
    d) Neither

7. In the sentence "He borrowed my computer," _____ is in the possessive case.
    a) He
    b) My
    c) Computer
    d) Borrowed

8. In the sentence "He borrowed my computer," _____ is in the objective case.
    a) He
    b) My
    c) Computer
    d) Borrowed

9. In the sentence "He borrowed my computer," _____ is in the subjective case.
    a) He
    b) My
    c) Computer
    d) Borrowed

10. "He," "it," and "her" are forms of the _____ singular personal pronoun.
   a) First person
   b) Second person
   c) Third person
   d) None of the above

ANSWER KEY

1. T, 2. T, 3. T, 4. F, 5. T, 6. c, 7. b, 8. c, 9. a, 10. c

CHAPTER 5

Greek Grammar: Nouns

You Should Know

- Stem: the basic form of a noun
- Case ending: the suffix added to the end of the stem of Greek nouns and adjectives that alters their form in relation to their function in the sentence
- Gloss: a rough approximation of what the Greek word means (not a translation)
- Parsing: indicates a noun's case, number, gender, lexical form, and perhaps other pieces of information, such as its meaning
- Lexical form: the nominative singular form of a noun
- Nominative case: indicates the subject of a verb
- Accusative case: indicates the direct object
- Dative case: indicates the indirect object
- Genitive case: functions much like the English word "of" and the possessive case
- Head noun: the word that the word in the genitive is modifying

Essay Questions

1. Copy a Greek verse from the New Testament or this unit's text and circle each pronoun, noun, and article.

2. Copy a Greek verse from the New Testament or this unit's text and circle anything in the nominative case.

Quiz

1. (T/F) The dative case is used to indicate the direct object.

2. (T/F) Greek words use inflection rather than word order to show a word's function.

3. (T/F) Greek nouns can be masculine, feminine, or neuter.

4. (T/F) Most Greek words follow natural gender.

5. (T/F) In the phrase "love of God," "God" is the head noun and "love" is in the genitive.

6. The basic form of a noun is called the:
   a) Lexical form
   b) Gloss
   c) Parsing
   d) Stem

7. Which of the following is a rough approximation of what a Greek word means?
   a) Lexical form
   b) Gloss
   c) Parsing
   d) Stem

8. Which of the following will tell you a noun's case, number, and gender (and perhaps other pieces of information, such as its meaning)?
   a) Lexical form
   b) Gloss
   c) Parsing
   d) Stem

9. The lexical form of a noun is its _____ singular form.
   a) Genitive
   b) Nominative
   c) Dative
   d) Accusative

10. The genitive case is:
    a) Descriptive
    b) Possessive
    c) Both
    d) Neither

ANSWER KEY
1. F, 2. T, 3. T, 4. F, 5. F, 6. d, 7. b, 8. c, 9. b, 10. c

CHAPTER 6

Prepositions

You Should Know

- Preposition: a word that indicates the relationship between a noun (or pronoun)
- and other words in the sentence
- Object of the preposition: the noun that follows the preposition
- Prepositional phrase: the preposition, its object, and any modifiers
- The preposition εἰς:
  - Ἐλθόντες **εἰς** τὴν οἰκίαν εἶδον τὸ παιδίον. (Matt 2:11)
    On coming to the house, they saw the child.
- The preposition ἐν:
  - Ἐβαπτίζοντο **ἐν** τῷ Ἰορδάνῃ ποταμῷ ὑπ᾽αὐτοῦ. (Matt 3:6)
    They were baptized by him in the river Jordan.
- The preposition ἀπό:
  - Νυνὶ δὲ κατηργήθημεν **ἀπὸ** τοῦ νόμου. (Rom 7:6)
    But now we have been released from the law.

Essay Questions

1. Describe various ways that you might use the preposition "in." What are the different meanings you can express with it?

2. Choose another preposition and describe the various ways that preposition might be used.

Quiz

1. (T/F) Prepositions and their objects form a prepositional phrase.

2. (T/F) The noun that follows the preposition is called the subject of the preposition.

3. (T/F) English requires the object of all prepositions to be in the objective case.

4. (T/F) The preposition controls the case of its object.

5. (T/F) Greek prepositions have a narrow range of meanings.

6. Which of the following indicates the relationship between a noun (or pronoun) and other words in the sentence?
    a) Preposition
    b) Prepositional phrase
    c) Object of the preposition
    d) None of the above

7. Some prepositions, like εἰς, take their object in the _____ case.
    a) Nominative
    b) Accusative
    c) Dative
    d) Genitive

8. Some prepositions, like ἀπό, take their object in the _____ case.
    a) Nominative
    b) Accusative
    c) Dative
    d) Genitive

9. Some prepositions, like ἐν, take their objects in the _____ case.
    a) Nominative
    b) Accusative
    c) Dative
    d) Genitive

10. No prepositions take their object in the _____ case.
   a) Nominative
   b) Accusative
   c) Dative
   d) Genitive

ANSWER KEY

1. T, 2. F, 3. T, 4. T, 5. F, 6. a, 7. b, 8. d, 9. c, 10. a

CHAPTER 7

English Grammar: Verb Inflection

You Should Know

- Verb: a word that describes an action or a state of being
- First person: the person speaking
- Second person: the person being spoken to
- Third person: that which is spoken about
- Voice: the relationship between a verb and its subject
- Mood: the relationship between the verb and reality
- Aspect: indicates what type of action a verb describes
- The three forms of tense into which English verbs divide: present, past, past participle
- The four moods: indicative, subjunctive, imperative, infinitive
- The three types of verbal aspect from this session: continuous, undefined, perfective

Essay Questions

1. What is the difference between tense and time in verbs? Give an example.

2. What is the difference between the indicative and subjunctive moods? Give an example.

Quiz

1. (T/F) A noun is a word that describes an action or a state of being.

2. (T/F) Aspect indicates what type of action a verb describes.

3. (T/F) In English the terms "tense" and "time" refer to the same thing.

4. (T/F) Mood refers to the relationship between the verb and reality.

5. (T/F) English verbs divide into three forms: the present, past, and future participle.

6. The _____ is the person speaking.
    a) First person
    b) Second person
    c) Third person
    d) None of the above

7. The _____ is that which is spoken about.
    a) First person
    b) Second person
    c) Third person
    d) None of the above

8. The _____ is the person being spoken to.
    a) First person
    b) Second person
    c) Third person
    d) None of the above

9. The _____ is the mood not of reality but of possibility or probability.
    a) Indicative
    b) Subjunctive
    c) Imperative
    d) Infinitive

10. The verb is in the _____ mood when it is making a command.
   a) Indicative
   b) Subjunctive
   c) Imperative
   d) Infinitive

ANSWER KEY

1. F, 2. T, 3. T, 4. T, 5. F, 6. a, 7. c, 8. b, 9. b, 10. c

CHAPTER 8

Greek Grammar: Verbs (Indicative)

You Should Know

- Personal ending: a suffix affixed to the end of a word that indicates person and number

- Morphology: the study of how a language uses small pieces of information (called "morphemes") to construct a word

- Lexical form: the first person singular, present indicative form of a verb as it appears in a dictionary

- The five tenses in Greek: present, future, imperfect, aorist, perfect

- The two Greek tenses that indicate past time: imperfect, aorist

- The present indicative:
  - Τινὲς δὲ καὶ δι' εὐδοκίαν τὸν Χριστὸν **κηρύσσουσιν**. (Phil 1:15)
    But others preach Christ out of goodwill.

- The future indicative:
  - Τὸ δὲ πνεῦμα ῥητῶς λέγει ὅτι ἐν ὑστέροις καιροῖς **ἀποστήσονταί** τινες. (1 Tim 4:1)
    Now the Spirit clearly says that in later times some will abandon the faith.

- The imperfect indicative:
  - Εἰσελθὼν εἰς τὴν συναγωγὴν **ἐδίδασκεν**. (Mark 1:21)
    He went into the synagogue and was teaching.

- The aorist indicative:
  - **Ἐγένετο** Ἰωάννης [ὁ] βαπτίζων ἐν τῇ ἐρήμῳ. (Mark 1:4)
    John the Baptist appeared in the wilderness.
- The perfect indicative:
  - Ἐποίησαν αὐτῷ ὅσα ἤθελον, καθὼς **γέγραπται** ἐπ' αὐτόν. (Mark 9:13)
    They have done to him whatever they wished, just as it is written about him.

Essay Questions

1. What does it mean to say aspect is more important than time?

2. What is the difference between the imperfect and the aorist tenses?

Quiz

1. (T/F) In Greek, "time" is more important than "aspect."

2. (T/F) A Greek verb must agree with its subject in person but not necessarily number.

3. (T/F) The lexical form of a verb is first person singular, present indicative.

4. (T/F) A paradigm is an overview of the different forms a word can take.

5. (T/F) There are five tenses in Greek: present, future, imperfect, aorist, and perfect.

6. The _____ is kind of like the default past tense.
    a) Aorist
    b) Imperfect
    c) Perfect
    d) None of the above

7. When the Bible says, "It is written," this is usually in the _____ tense.

   a) Aorist
   b) Imperfect
   c) Perfect
   d) None of the above

8. The _____ describes a continuous action that normally occurs in the past.

   a) Aorist
   b) Imperfect
   c) Perfect
   d) None of the above

9. The _____ describes an action that was brought to completion (and hence is usually in the past) but has effects felt in the speaker's present.

   a) Continunous aspect
   b) Undefined aspect
   c) Perfective aspect
   d) None of the above

10. A verb in the _____ describes something that is, as opposed to something that may or might be, or something that ought to be.

    a) Indicative
    b) Subjunctive
    c) Imperative
    d) Infinitive

ANSWER KEY

1. F, 2. F, 3. T, 4. T, 5. T, 6. a, 7. c, 8. b, 9. c, 10. a

CHAPTER 9

Greek Grammar: Verbs (Nonindicative)

You Should Know

- Once you are out of the indicative, the Greek verbal system has no time significance; it is all about aspect.

- The three voices of Greek: Active, Middle, Passive

- Deponent verb: a verb that is middle or passive in its form but active in its meaning

- The subjunctive:
  - Ἐὰν οὖν τις **ἐκκαθάρῃ** ἑαυτὸν ἀπὸ τούτων, ἔσται σκεῦος εἰς τιμήν. (2 Tim 2:21)
  Therefore, those who cleanse themselves from these will be instruments for special purposes.

- The second person imperative:
  - **Γύμναζε** δὲ σεαυτὸν πρὸς εὐσέβειαν. (1 Tim 4:7)
  Rather, train yourself to be godly.

- The third person infinitive:
  - **Ἐλθέτω** ἡ βασιλεία σου γενηθήτω τὸ θέλημά σου. (Matt 6:10)
  Your kingdom come, your will be done.

- The infinitive:
  - Ἤρξατο ὁ Ἰησοῦς **κηρύσσειν** καὶ λέγειν μετανοεῖτε. (Matt 4:17)
  Jesus began to preach and say, "Repent."

- The attributive participle:
  - Ἐὰν δὲ βραδύνω, ἵνα εἰδῇς πῶς δεῖ ἐν οἴκῳ θεοῦ ἀναστρέφεσθαι, ἥτις ἐστὶν ἐκκλησία θεοῦ **ζῶντος**. (1 Tim 3:15)
    If I am delayed, you will know how people ought to conduct themselves in God's household, which is the church of the living God.

- The adverbial participle:
  - Ἠλεήθην, ὅτι **ἀγνοῶν** ἐποίησα ἐν ἀπιστίᾳ. (1 Tim 1:13)
    I was shown mercy since, being ignorant, I had acted in unbelief.

- The substantival participle:
  - Χάριν ἔχω τῷ **ἐνδυναμώσαντί** με Χριστῷ Ἰησοῦ τῷ κυρίῳ ἡμῶν. (1 Tim 1:12)
    I thank Christ Jesus our Lord, who has given me strength.

Essay Questions

1. Give examples of an imperative in both the second person and third person.

2. Write a paragraph in which all the verbs are in the passive voice.

Quiz

1. (T/F) Outside the indicative, Greek verbs are concerned with aspect, not time.

2. (T/F) All Greek imperatives are second person; English has second and third person imperatives.

3. (T/F) If a verb is in the passive voice, it means the subject does the action of the verb.

4. (T/F) As a verbal adjective, a participle can function adjectivally or adverbially.

5. (T/F) As an adjective, a participle can function both as a normal adjective or a noun.

6. Verbal forms built on a stem in the _____ tense stem indicate an undefined action.

   a) Present
   b) Aorist
   c) Perfect
   d) Future

7. Verbal forms built on a stem in the _____ tense stem indicate a completed action.

   a) Present
   b) Aorist
   c) Perfect
   d) Future

8. Verbal forms built on a stem in the _____ tense stem indicate a continuous action.

   a) Present
   b) Aorist
   c) Perfect
   d) Future

9. Because the _____ is one step removed from reality, it is appropriate for purpose statements (purpose) and "if" clauses (conditional).

   a) Indicative
   b) Subjunctive
   c) Imperative
   d) Infinitive

10. The basic function of the _____ is to state a command.

    a) Indicative
    b) Subjunctive
    c) Imperative
    d) Infinitive

ANSWER KEY

1. T, 2. F, 3. F, 4. T, 5. T, 6. b, 7. c, 8. a, 9. b, 10. c

CHAPTER 10

Word Studies

You Should Know

- The steps in biblical word study:
    i. Choose the English word.
    ii. Identify the Greek word.
    iii. Discover the semantic range.
    iv. Explore the context.

- Cognate: a word related to another word that has the same root

- Semantic range: the possible meanings a word could possess

- Anachronism: equating a Greek word with a modern English word that shares that root

- Septuagint: the Greek translation of the Hebrew Scriptures begun around 250 BC and finished around the time of Christ

- All translation is interpretive.

- Etymological fallacy: the mistaken assumption that the etymology, the pieces ("morphemes") that were originally used to make up the word, define the word today

- For the most part, we do not communicate with individual words but with phrases, sentences, and paragraphs.

- κύριος: the Greek word "Lord" and the Hebrew word "Yahweh" (יהוה)

- ἔλεος: the Greek word "mercy" and the Hebrew word ḥesed, "steadfast love" (חֶסֶד)

Essay Questions

1. Do you agree or disagree with the statement "all translation is interpretive"? Why?

2. Is a word's etymology sufficient to explain its meaning? Why or why not?

Quiz

1. (T/F) Word study is essentially etymology.

2. (T/F) Often one word in one language will correspond exactly to another word in another language.

3. (T/F) A cognate is a word related to another word that has the same root.

4. (T/F) All translation is interpretive.

5. (T/F) The Septuagint is the Greek translation of the Hebrew Scriptures begun around 250 BC and finished around the time of Christ.

6. Which of the following refers to the possible meanings a word could possess?
   a) Anachronism
   b) Translation
   c) Semantic range
   d) None of the above

7. Equating a Greek word with a modern English word that shares that root is:
   a) Anachronism
   b) Translation
   c) Semantic range
   d) None of the above

8. At what point of word study might you be looking for often repeated words?
   a) Choose the English word
   b) Identify the Greek word

c) Discover its semantic range
d) Explore its context

9. At what point of word study would a Greek-English concordance be most useful?

a) Choose the English word
b) Identify the Greek word
c) Discover its semantic range
d) Explore its context

10. What word did New Testament authors use for "steadfast love"?

a) ἀγάπη
b) ἔλεος
c) κύριος
d) ἐμπλέκω

ANSWER KEY

1. F, 2. F, 3. T, 4. T, 5. T, 6. c, 7. a, 8. a, 9. c, 10. b

CHAPTER 11

Cases

You Should Know

- Accusative:
  - Καὶ εἶχον **ἰχθύδια** ὀλίγα. (Mark 8:7)
    They had a few small fish as well.
  - Εἶδεν Σίμωνα καὶ Ἀνδρέαν **τὸν ἀδελφὸν** Σίμωνος. (Mark 1:16)
    He saw Simon and Andrew the brother of Simon.
  - Ἐκεῖνος **ὑμᾶς** διδάξει **πάντα**. (John 14:26)
    He will teach you all things.

- Dative:
  - Μαριὰμ . . . ἐκμάξασα τοὺς πόδας αὐτοῦ **ταῖς θριξὶν** αὐτῆς. (John 11:2)
    Mary . . . wiped his feet with her hair.
  - Ἡ γυνή σου Ἐλισάβετ γεννήσει υἱόν **σοι**. (Luke 1:13)
    Your wife Elizabeth will bear you a son.
  - Ὕπαγε πρῶτον διαλλάγηθι **τῷ ἀδελφῷ** σου. (Matt 5:24)
    First go and be reconciled to your brother.

- Nominative:
  - Ἐγώ εἰμι ὁ **χριστός**. (Matt 24:5)
    I am the Christ.
  - Παῦλος **ἀπόστολος** Χριστοῦ Ἰησοῦ διὰ θελήματος θεοῦ (Eph 1:1)
    Paul, an apostle of Christ Jesus by the will of God

- Genitive:
  - Χάρις ὑμῖν καὶ εἰρήνη ἀπὸ θεοῦ **πατρὸς ἡμῶν**. (Col 1:2)
    Grace and peace to you from God our Father.
  - Οὐχὶ ἡ ψυχὴ πλεῖόν ἐστιν **τῆς τροφῆς**; (Matt 6:25)
    Is not life more than food?

Essay Question

1. Describe how Greek sentences indicate who the subject is. How do English sentences do the same?

Quiz

1. (T/F) A Greek sentence does not require an expressed subject.

2. (T/F) Simple apposition only occurs in the nominative.

3. (T/F) The dative is most commonly used in reference to direct objects.

4. (T/F) The subject of a sentence is in the nominative.

5. (T/F) In the object-complement category, one word will be the direct object and the second will predicate something about the direct object.

6. A verb agrees with its subject in:
   a) Person
   b) Number
   c) Both of the above
   d) None of the above

7. Which of the following is NOT a function of the dative?
   a) Locative
   b) Possessive
   c) Instrumental
   d) Proper

8. Which of the following is often used with comparative adjectives?
   a) Nominative
   b) Accusative
   c) Dative
   d) Genitive

9. Many times when English would use a preposition, Greek uses the:
   a) Nominative
   b) Accusative
   c) Dative
   d) Genitive

10. A head noun is found in _____ constructions.
    a) Nominative
    b) Accusative
    c) Dative
    d) Genitive

ANSWER KEY

1. T, 2. F, 3. F, 4. T, 5. T, 6. c, 7. b, 8. d, 9. c, 10. d

CHAPTER 12

Pronouns

You Should Know

- The first person singular pronouns in Greek for each case (non-emphatic form):
  - ἐγώ
  - μου
  - μοι
  - με

- The second person singular pronouns in Greek for each case (non-emphatic form):
  - σύ
  - σου
  - σοι
  - σε

- The third person masculine singular pronouns in Greek for each case:
  - αὐτος
  - αὐτοῦ
  - αὐτῷ
  - αὐτόν

- The third person feminine singular pronouns in Greek for each case:
  - αὐτή
  - αὐτῆς

- αὐτῇ
- αὐτήν
- The third person neuter singular pronouns in Greek for each case:
  - αὐτό
  - αὐτοῦ
  - αὐτῷ
  - αὐτό
- The first person plural pronouns in Greek for each case:
  - ἡμεῖς
  - ἡμῶν
  - ἡμῖν
  - ἡμᾶς
- The second person plural pronouns in Greek for each case:
  - ὑμεῖς
  - ὑμῶν
  - ὑμῖν
  - ὑμᾶς
- The third person masculine plural pronouns in Greek for each case:
  - αὐτοί
  - αὐτῶν
  - αὐτοῖς
  - αὐτούς
- The third person feminine plural pronouns in Greek for each case:
  - αὐταί
  - αὐτῶν
  - αὐταῖς
  - αὐτάς

Essay Questions

1. Why might a translator replace a pronoun with its antecedent?

2. Why might a Greek author use an emphatic pronoun such as ἐμοί instead of μοι? How would we make this distinction in English?

Quiz

1. (T/F) The case of a pronoun is determined by its function in the sentence.

2. (T/F) The number and person of a pronoun are determined by its function in a sentence.

3. (T/F) All personal pronouns can be singular or plural.

4. (T/F) The difference between emphatic and non-emphatic Greek pronouns is meaning.

5. (T/F) Translators sometimes replace a personal pronoun with its antecedent for the sake of clarity.

6. "I" is an example of a _____ pronoun.
    a) First person
    b) Second person
    c) Third person
    d) None of the above

7. "We" is an example of a _____ pronoun.
    a) First person
    b) Second person
    c) Third person
    d) None of the above

8. "You" is an example of a _____ pronoun.
    a) First person
    b) Second person
    c) Third person
    d) None of the above

9. Αὐτός is an example of a _____ pronoun.
   a) First person
   b) Second person
   c) Third person
   d) None of the above

10. There is gender in the:
    a) First person
    b) Second person
    c) Third person
    d) None of the above

ANSWER KEY

1. T, 2. F, 3. T, 4. F, 5. T, 6. a, 7. a, 8. b, 9. c, 10. c

CHAPTER 13

Modifiers

You Should Know

- The forms of the Greek masculine singular article as it appears in each case:
  - ὁ
  - τοῦ
  - τῷ
  - τόν

- The forms of the Greek feminine singular article as it appears in each case:
  - ἡ
  - τῆς
  - τῇ
  - τήν

- The forms of the Greek neuter singular article as it appears in each case:
  - ὁ
  - τοῦ
  - τῷ
  - τό

- The forms of the Greek masculine plural article as it appears in each case:
  - οἱ
  - τῶν

- τοῖς
- τούς

- The forms of the Greek feminine plural article as it appears in each case:
  - αἱ
  - τῶν
  - ταῖς
  - τάς

- The forms of the Greek neuter plural article as it appears in each case:
  - τά
  - τῶν
  - τοῖς
  - τά

- Adjective: a word that modifies a noun or pronoun

- Phrase: a group of related words that does not have a subject or a finite verb

- Elision: dropping the final vowel of a preposition and replacing it with an apostrophe for pronounciation

- Clause: a group of related words that contains a finite verb and its subject

Essay Questions

1. Why might ὁ be considered one of the most important Greek words?

2. What is the difference between a clause and a phrase? Give examples of each in English.

Quiz

1. (T/F) Greek often places articles in prepositional phrases where English would omit them.

2. (T/F) The object of a preposition will always be in the nominative.

3. (T/F) Relative pronouns get their gender and number from their antecedents, but their case from their function in a sentence.

4. (T/F) A "phrase" is a group of related words that does not have a subject or a finite verb.

5. (T/F) Clauses, unlike phrases, have a finite subject and verb.

6. Phrases can be categorized by:
   a) The word with which they begin
   b) Their function in the sentence
   c) Both of the above
   d) None of the above

7. Clauses are often connected by:
   a) Relative pronouns
   b) Prepositions
   c) Both of the above
   d) None of the above

8. Relative clauses can be:
   a) Attributive
   b) Substantival
   c) Both of the above
   d) None of the above

9. Which of the following is an example of an indefinite relative pronoun?
   a) We
   b) Over
   c) Him
   d) Whoever

10. The Greek relative pronoun is:
   a) ὁ
   b) ὅς
   c) αὐτός
   d) τό

ANSWER KEY

1. F, 2. F, 3. T, 4. T, 5. T, 6. c, 7. a, 8. c, 9. d, 10. b

CHAPTER 15

Verbal Aspect

You Should Know

- Aktionsart: the full meaning of a word in context
- Continuous action:
  - Οἱ ἀκολουθοῦντες **ἔκραζον** λέγοντες ὡσαννὰ τῷ υἱῷ Δαυίδ. (Matt 21:9)
  Those that followed were shouting, "Hosanna to the Son of David!"
- Undefined action:
  - Ἐλεήθην, ὅτι ἀγνοῶν **ἐποίησα** ἐν ἀπιστίᾳ. (1 Tim 1:13)
  I was shown mercy since, being ignorant, I had acted in unbelief.
- Perfective action:
  - **Ἠλπίκαμεν** ἐπὶ θεῷ ζῶντι, ὅς ἐστιν σωτὴρ πάντων ἀνθρώπων. (1 Tim 4:10)
  We have placed our hope in the living God, who is the Savior of all people.
- Instantaneous action:
  - Αἰνέα, **ἰᾶταί** σε Ἰησοῦς Χριστός . . . καὶ εὐθέως ἀνέστη. (Acts 9:34)
  Aeneas, Jesus Christ heals you . . . And immediately he got up.
- Ingressive action:
  - Ἐξαλλόμενος ἔστη καὶ **περιεπάτει** καὶ **εἰσῆλθεν** σὺν αὐτοῖς εἰς τὸ ἱερόν. (Acts 3:8)
  Jumping up, he stood and began to walk, and he entered the temple with them.

- Progressive action:
  - Εἰς τοῦτο γὰρ **κοπιῶμεν** καὶ **ἀγωνιζόμεθα**. (1 Tim 4:10)
    For with respect to this reason we are toiling and struggling.

- Customary action:
  - Τοιαύταις παραβολαῖς πολλαῖς **ἐλάλει** αὐτοῖς τὸν λόγον. (Mark 4:33)
    With many similar parables Jesus spoke the word to them.

- Gnomic action:
  - Πᾶς ὁ ἀρνούμενος τὸν υἱὸν οὐδὲ τὸν πατέρα **ἔχει**. (1 John 2:23)
    No one who denies the Son has the Father.

- Iterative action:
  - Ἐγὼ μὲν ὑμᾶς **βαπτίζω** ἐν ὕδατι εἰς μετάνοιαν. (Matt 3:11)
    I baptize you in water for repentance.

Essay Questions

1. Why is Aktionsart an important concept for understanding verbal aspect?

2. "In the Greek indicative, time is primary over aspect." Do you agree or disagree? Why?

Quiz

1. (T/F) Aktionsart is the full meaning of a word in context.

2. (T/F) Translators often add a word like "began" to clarify the progressive aspect.

3. (T/F) The indicative mood is used when the speaker wants to express something as reality.

4. (T/F) In the Greek indicative, time is primary over aspect.

5. (T/F) Lies cannot be expressed in the indicative.

6. Which of the following describes a completed action whose ongoing effects are felt in the present?

- a) Undefined
- b) Continuous
- c) Perfective
- d) None of the above

7. In which aspect does a verb tell you nothing about the nature of the action?

- a) Instantaneous
- b) Progressive
- c) Ingressive
- d) None of the above

8. Which of the following expresses timeless or axiomatic truths?

- a) Iterative
- b) Customary
- c) Gnomic
- d) None of the above

9. Which of the following means a verb's emphasis is on the beginning of an action?

- a) Ingressive
- b) Continuous
- c) Progressive
- d) None of the above

10. Which aspect refers to verbs that occur on a regular basis?

- a) Gnomic
- b) Progressive
- c) Customary
- d) None of the above

ANSWER KEY

1. T, 2. F, 3. T, 4. F, 5. F, 6. c, 7. d, 8. c, 9. a, 10. c

CHAPTER 16

Verbs (Voice)

You Should Know

- Active voice: The subject does the action of the verb.
- Passive voice: The subject receives the action of the verb.
- Middle voice: The subject does the action of the verb, but the subject is emphasized.
- Deponent verb: a verb that is passive in form but active in meaning
- Transitive verb: a verb that requires an object
- Intransitive verb: a verb that cannot have an object and cannot be passive
- Active:
  - Χριστὸς Ἰησοῦς **ἦλθεν** εἰς τὸν κόσμον ἁμαρτωλοὺς σῶσαι. (1 Tim 1:15)
    Christ Jesus came into the world to save sinners.
- Passive:
  - Οὗτος **ἐγενήθη** εἰς κεφαλὴν γωνίας. (Mark 12:10)
    He has become the chief cornerstone.
  - **Ἐβαπτίζοντο** ἐν τῷ Ἰορδάνῃ ποταμῷ ὑπ' αὐτοῦ. (Matt 3:6)
    They were being baptized in the Jordan River by him.
- Middle:
  - Εἰ υἱὸς εἶ τοῦ θεοῦ, **βάλε σεαυτὸν** κάτω. (Matt 4:6)
    If you are the Son of God, throw yourself down.

Essay Questions

1. What is the difference between the simple, causative, and stative uses of the active voice? Give an English example of each.

2. What is the difference between the direct and indirect uses of the middle voice? Give an English example of each.

Quiz

1. (T/F) A deponent verb has no active form, though it is active in meaning.

2. (T/F) When the subject performs the action of the verb through someone or something, the action is causative.

3. (T/F) While common in Koine Greek, the direct middle is rare in Classical Greek.

4. (T/F) The agent of an action must be expressed in the passive voice.

5. (T/F) Voice is the relationship between the verb and its subject.

6. Only the _____ voice tells us the subject that performs the action.
   a) Active
   b) Passive
   c) Middle
   d) All of the above

7. Which voice points back to the subject, asserting that the subject has a special interest in the action of the verb?
   a) Active
   b) Passive
   c) Middle
   d) All of the above

8. Which voice tells us that the subject receives the action of the verb?

    a) Active
    b) Passive
    c) Middle
    d) All of the above

9. Which of the following are defined by the relationship between the verb and its object?

    a) Transitive verbs
    b) Intransitive verbs
    c) Both of the above
    d) None of the above

10. Which of the following can be active, middle, or passive?

    a) Transitive verbs
    b) Intransitive verbs
    c) Both of the above
    d) None of the above

ANSWER KEY

1. T, 2. T, 3. F, 4. F, 5. T, 6. a, 7. c, 8. b, 9. c, 10. a

CHAPTER 17

Verbs (Tense)

You Should Know

- Present:
  - **Νηστεύω** δὶς τοῦ σαββάτου. (Luke 18:12)
    I fast twice a week.
  - Ἐὰν προσεύχωμαι γλώσσῃ, τὸ πνεῦμά μου **προσεύχεται**. (1 Cor 14:14)
    For if I pray in a tongue, my spirit prays.

- Future:
  - **Ἀγαπήσεις** κύριον τὸν θεόν σου. (Matt 22:37)
    You shall love the Lord your God.
  - Ὁ ἐναρξάμενος ἐν ὑμῖν ἔργον ἀγαθὸν **ἐπιτελέσει**. (Phil 1:6)
    He who began a good work in you will bring it to completion.

- Imperfect:
  - **Ἐδίδασκεν** τοὺς μαθητὰς αὐτοῦ. (Mark 9:31)
    He was teaching his disciples.
  - **Ἤρχοντο** πρὸς αὐτὸν καὶ **ἔλεγον** χαῖρε. (John 19:3)
    They were coming to him, saying "Hail!"

- Aorist:
  - Ὁ δὲ βασιλεὺς **ὠργίσθη**. (Matt 22:7)
    The king was angry.
  - **Ἐξηράνθη** ὁ χόρτος, καὶ τὸ ἄνθος **ἐξέπεσεν**. (1 Pet 1:24)
    The grass withers and the flower falls off.

- Perfect:
    - Ἄνθρωπε, **ἀφέωνταί** σοι αἱ ἁμαρτίαι σου. (Luke 5:20)
      Man, your sins are forgiven you.
    - Ἡ ἀγάπη τοῦ θεοῦ **ἐκκέχυται** ἐν ταῖς καρδίαις ἡμῶν. (Rom 5:5)
      God's love has been poured into our hearts.

Essay Questions

1. "The Greek verbal system views time as secondary to aspect." Do you agree or disagree? Why?

2. What are the differences between the aorist, the imperfect, and the perfect? Give English examples of each.

Quiz

1. (T/F) Greek sometimes makes the telling of the past more vivid by using the present tense.

2. (T/F) Another word for "linguistic sensitivity" is "interpretation."

3. (T/F) Unlike English, the Greek future cannot express a command.

4. (T/F) The Greek verb system views time as secondary to aspect.

5. (T/F) The aspect of the aorist tense is always defined.

6. When a Greek present tense describes an immediate action with no real continuous nature, it is:
    a) Instantaneous
    b) Aoristic
    c) Punctiliar
    d) All of the above

7. As a general rule, the future is translated with the _____ aspect.
    a) Undefined
    b) Continuous

c) Both of the above
d) None of the above

8. Which tense generally describes an ongoing action that happened in the past?

a) Present
b) Aorist
c) Imperfect
d) Perfect

9. Which tense describes a completed action whose results are felt in the present?

a) Present
b) Aorist
c) Imperfect
d) Perfect

10. When a verb is _____, the emphasis is on the completion of an event.

a) Constantive
b) Ingressive
c) Consummative
d) Gnomic

ANSWER KEY

1. T, 2. T, 3. F, 4. T, 5. F, 6. d, 7. a, 8. c, 9. d, 10. c

CHAPTER 18

Verbs (Nonindicative)

You Should Know

- A Greek verb has time significance only in the indicative. The only significance of a verb in the other moods is one of aspect.

- The four moods of a Greek verb: indicative, subjunctive, imperative, infinitive

- Indicative:
  - Ποῦ **ἐστιν** ὁ τεχθεὶς βασιλεὺς τῶν Ἰουδαίων; (Matt 2:2)
    Where is the one who is born king of the Jews?
  - Εἰ γὰρ Ἀβραὰμ ἐξ ἔργων **ἐδικαιώθη**, ἔχει καύχημα. (Rom 4:2)
    For if Abraham was justified by works, he has something to boast about.

- Subjunctive:
  - Ὃ ἂν **βλασφημήσῃ** εἰς τὸ πνεῦμα τὸ ἅγιον, οὐκ ἔχει ἄφεσιν εἰς τὸν αἰῶνα. (Mark 3:29)
    Whoever blasphemes against the Holy Spirit will never have forgiveness.
  - Ἐλεύσονται δὲ ἡμέραι ὅταν **ἀπαρθῇ** ἀπ' αὐτῶν ὁ νυμφίος. (Mark 2:20)
    But the days will come when the bridegroom will be taken from them.

- Imperative:
  - Κύριε, **δίδαξον** ἡμᾶς προσεύχεσθαι. (Luke 11:1)
    Lord, teach us to pray.
  - **Δότε** αὐτοῖς ὑμεῖς φαγεῖν. (Mark 6:37)
    You give them something to eat.

- Infinitive:
  - Μεταβαλόμενοι ἔλεγον αὐτὸν **εἶναι** θεόν. (Acts 28:6)
  They changed their minds and said that he was a god.
  - Ἐμοὶ τὸ **ζῆν** Χριστὸς καὶ τὸ **ἀποθανεῖν** κέρδος. (Phil 1:21)
  For to me, to live is Christ and to die is gain.

Essay Questions

1. What is the connection between time and the indicative?

2. What is the difference between the indicative, subjunctive, and imperative moods? Give an example of each.

Quiz

1. (T/F) A Greek verb has time significance only outside of the indicative.

2. (T/F) The indicative is used to ask a question.

3. (T/F) In hortatory statements, the translator will usually add words like "let us."

4. (T/F) The infinitive is often preceded by a masculine singular definite article when it is used as a substantive.

5. (T/F) Subjunctive statements that express purpose are usually introduced with ἵνα.

6. The imperative mood is used when a verb expresses a:
    a) Command
    b) Request
    c) Prohibition
    d) All of the above

7. The word _____ makes general statements with a subjunctive verb.
    a) ἄν
    b) ἐάν

c) Both of the above
d) None of the above

8. Forms built on the _____ stem indicate a continuous action.

   a) Present
   b) Aorist
   c) Perfect
   d) None of the above

9. When an infinitive completes the meaning of a finite verb, its function is:

   a) Declarative
   b) Complementary
   c) Interrogative
   d) Imperatival

10. A common way of indicating the result of some action is to use a clause introduced by:

   a) ἄν
   b) ἐάν
   c) ὥστε
   d) ἵνα

ANSWER KEY

1. F, 2. T, 3. T, 4. F, 5. T, 6. d, 7. c, 8. a, 9. b, 10. c

CHAPTER 19

Participles

You Should Know

- Participle: a verbal adjective that can modify either a noun (adjectival) or a verb (adverbial)
- The aorist participle describes an action without commenting on the nature of the action.
- The present participle describes a continuous action.
- The perfect participle describes a completed action with present effects.
- Adjectival:
  - Πάντα δυνατὰ τῷ **πιστεύοντι**. (Mark 9:23)
    All things are possible for one who believes.
  - Πᾶς ὁ **ἔχων** τὴν ἐλπίδα ταύτην ἐπ' αὐτῷ ἁγνίζει ἑαυτόν. (1 John 3:3)
    Everyone who thus hopes in him purifies himself.
  - Καὶ **παράγων** ὁ Ἰησοῦς ἐκεῖθεν εἶδεν ἄνθρωπον. (Matt 9:9)
    And Jesus, as he was passing on from there, saw a man.
- Adverbial:
  - **Νηστεύσας** . . . ὕστερον ἐπείνασεν. (Matt 4:2)
    After fasting . . . he was hungry.
  - Κοπιῶμεν **ἐργαζόμενοι** ταῖς ἰδίαις χερσίν. (1 Cor 4:12)
    We toil by working with our own hands.
  - Πάντα ὅσα ἂν αἰτήσητε . . . **πιστεύοντες** λήμψεσθε. (Matt 21:22)
    And all things you ask in prayer . . . believing, you will receive.

Essay Questions

1. What is the difference between a participle's adjectival and adverbial functions? Give examples of each.

2. What is a participial phrase? Give an example of one.

Quiz

1. (T/F) The primary significance of participles is one of tense.

2. (T/F) A participle is a verbal adjective.

3. (T/F) Since an adjective can also function as a noun, so can a participle.

4. (T/F) Most adjectival participles are nominative to match the subject of the verb.

5. (T/F) The participle built on the aorist tense stem indicates an action occurring at the same time as the time of the main verb.

6. Which participles modify some other noun or pronoun in the sentence and agree with that word in case, number, and gender?
    a) Adverbial
    b) Adjectival
    c) Both of the above
    d) None of the above

7. Which participles are usually preceded by ὁ?
    a) Adverbial
    b) Adjectival
    c) Both of the above
    d) None of the above

8. Which participles are usually anarthrous?
    a) Adverbial
    b) Adjectival
    c) Both of the above
    d) None of the above

9. Which participles describe an action without commenting on the nature of the action?
   a) Aorist
   b) Present
   c) Perfect
   d) None of the above

10. Which participles describe a completed action with present effects?
    a) Aorist
    b) Present
    c) Perfect
    d) None of the above

ANSWER KEY

1. F, 2. T, 3. T, 4. F, 5. F, 6. b, 7. b, 8. a, 9. a, 10. c

CHAPTER 20

Conjunctions

You Should Know

- Coordinating conjunctions connect grammatically equal units.
- Subordinate conjunctions begin a dependent clause and often link it to an independent clause.
- ἀλλά: coordinating conjunction
- οὖν: coordinating conjunction
- ὅτι: subordinate conjunction
- ἵνα: subordinate conjunction
- εἰ: subordinate conjuction
- μέν . . . δέ: correlative conjunctions
- ἤ . . . ἤ: correlative conjunctions

Essay Questions

1. Why are conjunctions important for translation, exegesis, and general reading?

2. Explain how coordinating, subordinate, and correlative conjunctions each function. Give an example in both Greek and English.

Quiz

1. (T/F) Almost every sentence in Greek narrative begins with a conjunction.

2. (T/F) Correlative conjunctions connect grammatically equal units.

3. (T/F) Subordinate conjunctions begin a dependent clause and often link it to an independent clause.

4. (T/F) Coordinating conjunctions work in pairs.

5. (T/F) Greek conjunctions are nuanced and have very distinct meanings.

6. Ὅς is an example of a:
   a) Coordinating conjunction
   b) Subordinate conjunction
   c) Correlative conjunction
   d) None of the above

7. Εἰ is an example of a:
   a) Coordinating conjunction
   b) Subordinate conjunction
   c) Correlative conjunction
   d) None of the above

8. Ἀλλά is an example of a:
   a) Coordinating conjunction
   b) Subordinate conjunction
   c) Correlative conjunction
   d) None of the above

9. Ὅτι is an example of a:
   a) Coordinating conjunction
   b) Subordinate conjunction
   c) Correlative conjunction
   d) None of the above

10. Μέν . . . δέ is an example of a:
    a) Coordinating conjunction
    b) Subordinate conjunction
    c) Correlative conjunction
    d) None of the above

ANSWER KEY

1. T, 2. F, 3. T, 4. F, 5. F, 6. d, 7. b, 8. a, 9. b, 10. c

CHAPTER 22

Pronouns

You Should Know

- Emphatic form: the form of a personal pronoun used when the author wants to emphasize the person in the sentence, often to contrast one person with another

- The three emphatic forms of the first person personal Greek pronoun: ἐμοῦ, ἐμοί, ἐμέ

- The three emphatic forms of the second person personal Greek pronoun: σοῦ, σοί, σέ

- The demonstrative pronoun, "this" or "these":
  - Εἰπὲ ἵνα οἱ λίθοι **οὗτοι** ἄρτοι γένωνται. (Matt 4:3)
    Tell these stones to become bread.

- A pronoun functioning as an identical adjective, "same":
  - Καὶ πάλιν ἀπελθὼν προσηύξατο **τὸν αὐτὸν** λόγον. (Mark 14:39)
    And again he went away and prayed the same thing.

- The collective pronoun, "all":
  - θεοῦ ... ὃς **πάντας** ἀνθρώπους θέλει σωθῆναι. (1 Tim 2:3–4)
    God ... who wants all people to be saved.

- An example of the demonstrative pronoun, "that" or "those":
  - **Ἐκείνοις** δὲ οὐ δέδοται. (Matt 13:11)
    But to them it has not been given.

- The collective pronoun, "whole":
  - οὓς δεῖ ἐπιστομίζειν, οἵτινες **ὅλους** οἴκους ἀνατρέπουσιν (Titus 1:11)
    who must be silenced, because they are disrupting whole families

- The intensive pronoun, "himself":
  - **Αὐτὸς** γὰρ ὁ Ἡρῴδης ἀποστείλας ἐκράτησεν τὸν Ἰωάννην. (Mark 6:17)
  For Herod himself had given orders to have John arrested.

- The possessive pronoun, "his":
  - Παρέλαβεν τὸ παιδίον καὶ τὴν μητέρα **αὐτοῦ** νυκτὸς. (Matt 2:14)
  He took the child and his mother during the night.

Essay Questions

1. What is the difference between an enclitic and a proclitic?

2. What are the three different uses of αὐτός?

Quiz

1. (T/F) Greek authors often use the emphatic form of pronouns often when they wish to contrast one person with another.

2. (T/F) The closest English comes to αὐτός is the reflexive pronoun.

3. (T/F) If a demonstrative is functioning as an adjective, it will be anarthrous.

4. (T/F) Οὗτος is sometimes used as the identical adjective meaning "same."

5. (T/F) Αὐτός does not agree with the noun it modifies in case, number, and gender.

6. The most common use of _____ is as the third person personal pronoun.
   a) αὐτός
   b) οὗτος
   c) ἐκεῖνος
   d) None of the above

7. The demonstrative pronoun that means "that" or "those" is:
   a) αὐτός
   b) οὗτος
   c) ἐκεῖνος
   d) None of the above

8. The demonstrative pronoun that means "this" or "these" is:
   a) αὐτός
   b) οὗτος
   c) ἐκεῖνος
   d) None of the above

9. Which of the following is sometimes used as the identical adjective meaning "same"?
   a) αὐτός
   b) οὗτος
   c) ἐκεῖνος
   d) None of the above

10. Which forms of αὐτός, such as αὐτοῦ and αὐτῶν, indicate possession?
    a) Nominative
    b) Accustive
    c) Dative
    d) Genitive

ANSWER KEY

1. T, 2. T, 3. T, 4. F, 5. F, 6. a, 7. c, 8. b, 9. a, 10. d

CHAPTER 23

Definite Article, and Odds 'n Ends

You Should Know

- Diaeresis: a diacritical mark (¨) placed over the second of two vowels that shows they are to be pronounced separately

- Subject: the subject of the main verb and anything that modifies it

- Predicate: anything in a sentence except the subject and its modifiers

- Postpositive: a word that cannot occur as the first word in the Greek clause (e.g., γάρ, δέ, and οὖν).

- Simple sentence: a sentence with one subject and one verb

- Compound sentence: a sentence that has two or more independent clauses connected with a coordinating conjunction or punctuation

- Complex sentence: a sentence that has one independent clause and one (or more) dependent clauses

- Compound-complex sentence: a sentence that has two (or more) independent clauses and one (or more) dependent clauses

- Idiom: a collection of words (usually two) that have a special meaning when the words occur together, a meaning that the words don't have when they are isolated

- Noun phrase: a phrase that is not prepositional or participial, but conveys a consistent meaning between nouns

Essay Questions

1. What are the differences between simple, compound, complex, and compound-complex sentences?

2. What is a noun phrase? Give an example.

Quiz

1. (T/F) Greek is a paratactic language, which is linear and prefers to use linked independent clauses over a series of dependent clauses and modifiers.

2. (T/F) In a general sense, the normal Greek word order is: conjunction, verb, subject, object.

3. (T/F) Older grammars and some modern commentaries list the infinitive form as the lexical form (e.g., λέγειν, "to say").

4. (T/F) The predicate is the subject of the main verb and anything that modifies it.

5. (T/F) Ὁ actually has one of the widest ranges of meaning of all Greek words.

6. Which of the following is an example of elision?
   a) Ἠσαΐας
   b) καὶ
   c) ἀλλ'
   d) None of the above

7. Which of the following is an example of diaeresis?
   a) Ἠσαΐας
   b) καὶ
   c) ἀλλ'
   d) None of the above

8. Which of the following is an example of punctuation changing an accent?
   a) Ἠσαΐας
   b) καὶ

c) ἀλλ'
d) None of the above

9. What kind of sentence has one independent clause and one or more dependent clauses?

   a) Simple sentence
   b) Compound sentence
   c) Complex sentence
   d) Compound-complex sentence

10. Which of the following is a postpositive?

    a) γάρ
    b) δέ
    c) οὖν
    d) All of the above

ANSWER KEY

1. F, 2. T, 3. T, 4. F, 5. T, 6. c, 7. a, 8. b, 9. c, 10. d

CHAPTER 24

Adjectives

You Should Know

- Articular: when a word is preceded by the definite article (ὁ)
- Anarthrous: when a word is not preceded by the definite article (ὁ)
- First attributive postion:
  - ἀπὸ **τῆς πρώτης ἡμέρας** ἄχρι τοῦ νῦν (Phil 1:5)
    from the first day until now
- Second attributive position:
  - τὸ πνεῦμα τὸ ἅγιον
    the Holy Spirit
- First predicate position:
  - **Μακάριοι οἱ εἰρηνοποιοί.** (Matt 5:9)
    Blessed are the peacemakers.
- Second predicate position:
  - Χαίρετε καὶ ἀγαλλιᾶσθε, ὅτι **ὁ μισθὸς ὑμῶν πολὺς**. (Matt 5:12)
    Rejoice and be glad, because your reward is great.
- The substantival function of the adjective:
  - Ἰωσὴφ δὲ ὁ ἀνὴρ αὐτῆς, **δίκαιος** ὤν (Matt 1:19)
    Now Joseph her husband, being a righteous man
- Superlative: μέγιστος
- Positive: μέγας
- Comparative: μείζων

Essay Questions

1. What does it mean to say, "Greek adjectives can function substantively"?

2. What is the difference between positive, comparative, and superlative degrees? Give examples of each.

Quiz

1. (T/F) When an adjective functions substantively, it functions as if it were a noun.

2. (T/F) Attributive adjectives tend to be articular; predicate adjectives are anarthrous.

3. (T/F) Adjectives can appear in the predicate, which means they occur after the verb.

4. (T/F) If a word is preceded by ὁ, the word is anarthrous.

5. (T/F) In Koine the comparative was dying out and its function was being assumed by the positive.

6. An example of the first predicate position is:
    a) Article–modifier–substantive
    b) Article–noun–article–adjective
    c) Adjective–article–noun
    d) Article–noun–adjective

7. An example of the second attributive position is:
    a) Article–modifier–substantive
    b) Article–noun–article–adjective
    c) Adjective–article–noun
    d) Article–noun–adjective

8. Which of the following denotes the greater of two items ("larger," μείζων)?
    a) Superlative degree
    b) Positive degree

c) Comparative degree
d) None of the above

9. Which of the following is the uncompared form of the adjective ("large," μέγας)?

    a) Superlative degree
    b) Positive degree
    c) Comparative degree
    d) None of the above

10. Which of the following describes the greatest or makes a comparison of three or more ("largest," μέγιστος)?

    a) Superlative degree
    b) Positive degree
    c) Comparative degree
    d) None of the above

ANSWER KEY

1. T, 2. T, 3. T, 4. F, 5. F, 6. c, 7. b, 8. c, 9. b, 10. a

CHAPTER 25

Phrases and Clauses

You Should Know

- A relative clause without an example of attraction:
  - Μέσος ὑμῶν ἕστηκεν **ὃν** ὑμεῖς οὐκ οἴδατε. (John 1:26)
    But among you stands one you do not know.

- A prepositional phrase that drops its article:
  - Ἁμαρτία ἦν **ἐν κόσμῳ**. (Rom 5:13)
    Sin was in the world.

- A participial phrase functioning substantivally:
  - Μακάριοι οἱ **πενθοῦντες**, ὅτι αὐτοὶ παρακληθήσονται. (Matt 5:4)
    Blessed are those who mourn, for they will be comforted.

- An example of a participial phrase functioning attributively:
  - φωνὴ ἐν Ῥαμὰ ἠκούσθη . . . Ῥαχὴλ **κλαίουσα** τὰ τέκνα αὐτῆς. (Matt 2:18)
    A voice is heard in Ramah . . . Rachel weeping for her children.

- A relative clause with an example of attraction:
  - ἤγγιζεν ὁ χρόνος τῆς ἐπαγγελίας **ἧς** ὡμολόγησεν ὁ θεὸς τῷ Ἀβραάμ (Acts 7:17)
    As the time drew near for God to fulfill his promise to Abraham

- A prepositional phrase acting as a modifier to a noun:
  - Ἐχαρίσατο αὐτῷ τὸ ὄνομα **τὸ ὑπὲρ πᾶν ὄνομα**. (Phil 2:9)
    He gave him the name that is above every name.

- More probable future third class condition:
  - Ἐὰν ἅψωμαι κἂν τῶν ἱματίων αὐτοῦ σωθήσομαι. (Matt 4:9)
    If I can only touch his clothes, I will be healed.

- Present general third class condition:
  - Ἐάν τις περιπατῇ ἐν τῇ ἡμέρᾳ, οὐ προσκόπτει. (John 11:9)
    If anyone walks in the day, he does not stumble.

- Second class condition:
  - Εἰ γὰρ ἐπιστεύετε Μωϋσεῖ, ἐπιστεύετε ἂν ἐμοί. (John 5:46)
    If you believed Moses, you would believe me.

- First class condition:
  - Εἰ υἱὸς εἶ τοῦ θεοῦ, εἰπὲ τῷ λίθῳ τούτῳ ἵνα γένηται ἄρτος. (Luke 4:3)
    If you are the Son of God, command this stone to become a loaf of bread.

Essay Questions

1. What is the difference between a participial and prepositional phrase?

2. Why might a translator break a long Greek sentence into multiple English sentences based on its relative clauses?

Quiz

1. (T/F) A prepositional phrase cannot act as a modifier.

2. (T/F) Like adjectives, an articular prepositional phrase can function substantivally.

3. (T/F) The "if" clause is called the protasis; the "then" clause is the apodosis.

4. (T/F) Attraction is when the relative pronoun is altered to be the same case as its antecedent.

5. (T/F) Greek writers always keep pronouns and their antecedents close together.

6. When used with ὁ, the participial phrase will normally be in the:
   a) First attributive position
   b) Second attributive position
   c) First predicate position
   d) Second predicate position

7. Relative pronouns can be changed to indefinite relative pronouns, (e.g., "whoever, whichever, whatever") when they are followed by:
   a) ἄν
   b) ἐάν
   c) Both of the above
   d) None of the above

8. Conditional statements "contrary to fact" begin with εἰ and a past tense verb in which mood?
   a) Indicative
   b) Imperative
   c) Subjunctive
   d) None of the above

9. Third class conditional statements begin with ἐάν and a verb in which mood?
   a) Indicative
   b) Imperative
   c) Subjunctive
   d) None of the above

10. Attraction does NOT happen because:
    a) The relative pronoun occurs in the immediate proximity to the antecedent
    b) The gender of the relative pronoun's antecedent is masculine
    c) The relative pronoun normally would be accusative
    d) The antecedent is dative or genitive

ANSWER KEY

1. F, 2. T, 3. T, 4. T, 5. F, 6. b, 7. c, 8. a, 9. c, 10. b

CHAPTER 27

Nouns

You Should Know

- The eight possible cases in Greek: nominative, accusative, dative, genitive, locative, instrumental, vocative, ablative

- Nominative:
    - Ἡ **παῖς**, ἔγειρε. (Luke 8:54)
    Child, get up!

- Accusative:
    - **ὃν** οὐκ ἰδόντες ἀγαπᾶτε (1 Pet 1:8)
    whom you have not seen, you love

    - Ζητεῖτε **πρῶτον** τὴν βασιλείαν τοῦ θεοῦ. (Matt 6:33)
    Seek first the kingdom of God.

    - Dative: **αρρησίᾳ** λαλεῖ. (John 7:26)
    He is speaking publicly.

    - Ἐγὼ δὲ **λιμῷ** ὧδε ἀπόλλυμαι. (Luke 15:17)
    But here I am dying with hunger!

    - Μὴ γίνεσθε ἑτεροζυγοῦντες **ἀπίστοις**. (2 Cor 6:14)
    Do not be unequally yoked with unbelievers.

- Genitive:
    - εἰ δέ τινες **τῶν κλάδων** ἐξεκλάσθησαν (Rom 11:17)
    if some of the branches have been broken off

    - πάντες οἱ θησαυροὶ **τῆς σοφίας καὶ γνώσεως** (Col 2:3)
    all the treasures of wisdom and knowledge

- Vocative:
    - Ὁ Ἰησοῦς εἶπεν αὐτῇ, **ὦ γύναι**, μεγάλη σου ἡ πίστις. (Matt 15:28)
    Jesus said to her, "Woman, great is your faith!"

Essay Questions

1. Does Greek have four or eight cases? Why?

2. How many cases does English have? Why?

Quiz

1. (T/F) A declension is the smallest amount of information in a word.

2. (T/F) A morpheme is a basic pattern for inflecting a noun or adjective.

3. (T/F) Greek often includes a verb's direct object, which is often removed in English.

4. (T/F) The basic idea of the ablative case is "from."

5. (T/F) If categorized by form, Greek has eight cases; if by meaning, Greek has four.

6. Declensions have to do with:
    a) Form
    b) Meaning
    c) Both of the above
    d) None of the above

7. An ὦ may be added in the _____ case if there is deep emotion or emphasis.
    a) Nominative
    b) Ablative
    c) Vocative
    d) Instrumental

8. After comparative adjectives (πολύς, ἰσχυρός, etc.) you will often find a word in the:
   a) Genitive
   b) Accustive
   c) Dative
   d) Instrumental

9. The locative and instrumental tenses are often expressed by the _____ case.
   a) Nominative
   b) Accusative
   c) Dative
   d) Genitive

10. Which of the following is an example of a word that would never be inflected?
   a) αὐτός
   b) Ἀβραάμ
   c) Ἰησοῦς
   d) ἐπιθυμεῖ

ANSWER KEY
1. F, 2. F, 3. F, 4. T, 5. F, 6. a, 7. c, 8. a, 9. c, 10. b

CHAPTER 28

Verbs (Indicative)

You Should Know

- Present:
  - Χριστὸς ἐγερθεὶς ἐκ νεκρῶν οὐκέτι **ἀποθνῄσκει**. (Rom 6:9)
    Since Christ was raised from the dead, he cannot die again.
  - Ἤγγικεν ἡ ὥρα καὶ ὁ υἱὸς τοῦ ἀνθρώπου **παραδίδοται**. (Matt 26:45)
    The hour has come, and the Son of Man is betrayed.

- Future:
  - Οὐκ ἐπ' ἄρτῳ μόνῳ **ζήσεται** ὁ ἄνθρωπος. (Matt 4:4)
    Man shall not live on bread alone.

- Imperfect:
  - **Ηὐχόμην** γὰρ ἀνάθεμα εἶναι αὐτὸς ἐγώ. (Rom 9:3)
    For I could wish that I myself were cursed.
  - **Ἐδίωκον** τὴν ἐκκλησίαν τοῦ θεοῦ καὶ ἐπόρθουν αὐτήν. (Gal 1:13)
    I persecuted the church of God and tried to destroy it.
  - Ὁ δὲ Ἰωάννης **διεκώλυεν** αὐτόν. (Matt 3:14)
    But John tried to deter him.

- Aorist:
  - Εἴ τις θέλει ὀπίσω μου ἔρχεσθαι, ἀρνησάσθω ἑαυτὸν καὶ **ἀράτω** τὸν σταυρὸν αὐτοῦ καθ' ἡμέραν, καὶ ἀκολουθείτω μοι. (Luke 9:23)
    Whoever wants to come after me must deny themselves and take up their cross daily and follow me.

- Passive:
  - Μακάριοι οἱ πενθοῦντες, ὅτι αὐτοὶ **παρακληθήσονται**. (Matt 5:4)
    Blessed are those who mourn, for they will be comforted.
  - Μετὰ τρεῖς ἡμέρας **ἐγείρομαι**. (Matt 27:63)
    After three days I will rise again.
- Neuter plural:
  - **Τὰ ἀρχαῖα** παρῆλθεν, ἰδοὺ γέγονεν καινά. (2 Cor 5:17)
    The old has gone, the new is here!

Essay Questions

1. Why might an author use the present tense to describe future events? Give an example.

2. What different senses can be expressed with the Greek imperfect tense?

Quiz

1. (T/F) The stem is the part of the verb that carries its basic meaning.

2. (T/F) English favors passive verbs, so many Greek actives become passive in translation.

3. (T/F) Some tenses add a letter such as σ or κ to a word's stem before the rest of the word.

4. (T/F) Greek often adds a connecting vowel between the stem of a verb and its personal ending to aid in pronunciation.

5. (T/F) Common verbs occasionally utilize different stems between tenses.

6. The imperfect does NOT describe:
    a) What a person wishes to do
    b) What a person tries to do

c) What a person will do
d) What a person almost does

7. English speakers commonly mistake the Greek _____ for the punctiliar past.

    a) Present
    b) Aorist
    c) Imperfect
    d) Perfect

8. Sometimes Greek utilizes the _____ tense to refer to future events.

    a) Present
    b) Aorist
    c) Imperfect
    d) Perfect

9. Which of the following is an example of an augment?

    a) ἀγαπήσω
    b) λέγετε
    c) λύεις
    d) ἔλεγεν

10. A subject that is _____ can have a singular verb when the subject is being viewed as a collective whole.

    a) Masculine plural
    b) Feminine plural
    c) Neuter plural
    d) None of the above

ANSWER KEY

1. T, 2. F, 3. T, 4. T, 5. T, 6. c, 7. b, 8. a, 9. d, 10. c

CHAPTER 29

Verbs (Nonindicative)

You Should Know

- Prohibition:
  - **Οὐκ ἐκπειράσεις** κύριον τὸν θεόν σου. (Matt 4:7)
    Do not put the Lord your God to the test.
  - **Μὴ φοβηθῇς** παραλαβεῖν Μαρίαν τὴν γυναῖκά σου. (Matt 1:20)
    Do not be afraid to take Mary as your wife.

- Emphatic negation:
  - Οἱ λόγοι μου **οὐ μὴ παρέλθωσιν**. (Matt 24:35)
    My words will never pass away.

- Question:
  - **Ποῦ ἐστιν** ὁ τεχθεὶς βασιλεὺς τῶν Ἰουδαίων; (Matt 2:2)
    Where is the one who has been born king of the Jews?
  - **Τί φάγωμεν;** ἤ **τί πίωμεν;** ἤ **τί περιβαλώμεθα;** (Matt 6:31)
    "What shall we eat?" or "What shall we drink?" or "What shall we wear?"

- Optative:
  - Ἁμαρτήσωμεν, ὅτι οὐκ ἐσμὲν ὑπὸ νόμον ἀλλὰ ὑπὸ χάριν; **μὴ γένοιτο**. (Rom 6:15)
    Shall we sin because we are not under the law but under grace? By no means!

- Imperative:
  - **Μετανοεῖτε** ἤγγικεν γὰρ ἡ βασιλεία τῶν οὐρανῶν. (Matt 3:2)
    Repent, for the kingdom of heaven is near.

- Infinitive:
  - Περισσόν μοί ἐστιν **τὸ γράφειν** ὑμῖν. (2 Cor 9:1)
  There is no need for me to write to you.

- Adverbial participle:
  - **Ἀκούσας** δὲ ὁ βασιλεὺς Ἡρῴδης ἐταράχθη. (Matt 2:3)
  When King Herod heard this he was disturbed.
  - Τῇ γὰρ χάριτί **ἐστε σεσῳσμένοι** διὰ πίστεως. (Eph 2:8)
  For it is by grace you have been saved, through faith.

Essay Question

1. What are some different ways a Greek author might express a prohibition, an imperative, and ask a question? Give examples.

Quiz

1. (T/F) The form of a Greek participle depends on whether it is adjectival or adverbial.

2. (T/F) The optative is sometimes called the mood of "wish."

3. (T/F) Greek utilizes helping verbs more often than English.

4. (T/F) It is uncommon for Greek to have an indicative verb accompanied by a redundant participle with the same basic meaning.

5. (T/F) The infinitive is always indeclinable.

6. With which of the following can Greek ask a question that expects the answer "Yes."
   a) μή
   b) οὐ
   c) οὐ μή
   d) μὴ γένοιτο

7. Which of the following is NOT a way of expressing a command in Greek?

a) Future indicative
   b) Present imperative
   c) Perfect indicative
   d) Aorist Imperative

8. A periphrastic construction uses _____ and a participle to state a single idea.

   a) εἰμί
   b) οὐχί
   c) ἔχω
   d) ἔρχομαι

9. Which of the following does NOT indicate time with the infinitive?

   a) ἐν
   b) μετά
   c) εἰς
   d) πρό

10. Which of the following does NOT express purpose with the infinitive?

   a) Infinitive with an article in the genitive case (τοῦ)
   b) πρὸς τό and the infinitive
   c) The simple infinitive
   d) διά and the infinitive

ANSWER KEY

1. F, 2. T, 3. F, 4. F, 5. T, 6. b, 7. c, 8. a, 9. c, 10. d

CHAPTER 31

The History of the Bible and Textual Criticism

You Should Know

- Harmonization: the process of making sure the gospels agree with one another

- Textus Receptus: a popular edition of Desiderius Erasmus's Bible

- William Tyndale: the first to translate the Bible into English from Greek and Hebrew

- Vulgate: Jerome's Latin translation of the Bible from Greek and Hebrew

- Tertullian: an early church father who had a Latin Bible as early as AD 160

- Complutensian Polyglot Bible: an interlinear Bible with Hebrew, Aramaic, Greek, and Latin

- John Wycliffe: "The Morning Star of the Reformation," who translated the Vulgate into English

- Textual Criticism: the science of studying the differences among manuscripts and deciding which reading is most likely to be original

- Marcion: the heretic who tried to remove all Jewishness from Jesus and the New Testament

- Lucian: the major compiler of an early, edited version of the Greek New Testament

Essay Questions

1. How can a translation of Scripture into another language (Greek, Latin, Aramaic, etc.) and textual criticism both aid our understanding of Scripture?

2. What does it mean to say, "Manuscripts are not to be counted but weighed"?

Quiz

1. (T/F) The epistles were originally written to clarify general Christian truths for all people.

2. (T/F) Intentional changes in manuscripts by New Testament scribes were ill-intentioned.

3. (T/F) Many manuscripts of the Greek New Testament are identical.

4. (T/F) The Eastern Church used Greek, while the Western Church used Latin.

5. (T/F) The Vulgate is a Latin translation of the Bible.

6. Which of the following is a NOT a reason the Gospels differ?
    a) They were intended for different audiences
    b) Their authors each had his own style
    c) They were written centuries apart
    d) They each have different themes

7. The process of making sure the Gospels agree with one another is called:
    a) Exegesis
    b) Harmonization
    c) Textual criticism
    d) Hermeneutics

8. Who had a Latin Bible as early as AD 160?
    a) Tertullian
    b) Marcion

c) Lucian
d) Jerome

9. Which of the following was a popular edition of Desiderius Erasmus' Bible?

   a) Geneva Bible
   b) Textus Receptus
   c) Complutensian Polyglot Bible
   d) Vulgate

10. Who was the first to translate the Bible into English from Greek and Hebrew?

    a) John Wycliffe
    b) Henry VIII
    c) King James
    d) William Tyndale

ANSWER KEY

1. F, 2. F, 3. F, 4. T, 5. T, 6. c, 7. b, 8. a, 9. b, 10. d

CHAPTER 32

Translations

You Should Know

- Dynamic equivalence: a tendency in translation that favors meaning over literal form

- Formal equivalence: a tendency in translation that favors literal form over meaning

- Passive vocabulary: the words one might not use but does understand

- Audience: those who will read and hear the text and whose concerns and circumstances inform the translation of a text

- Ambiguity: when the biblical text is decidedly unclear or open to multiple meanings

- Euphemism: changing the language of Scripture to a form that would be more socially acceptable to certain audiences

- Theological biases: the theological assumptions that affect one's translation or interpretation of the Bible

- Inclusive language: the removal of masculine or patriarchal language in the Bible, or the addition of language that includes feminine or collective emphases

- The Message: the New Testament translation that most exemplies dynamic equivalence

- Interlinear: the New Testament translation that most exemplies formal equivalence

Essay Questions

1. Why might word-for-word translations end up being more interpretive than literal?

2. Should euphemisms be used in translation, or should we adjust ourselves more to the Bible's language?

Quiz

1. (T/F) The most basic question in translation is, "Am I going to translate words or meaning?"

2. (T/F) Translating a text word-for-word is the best way to eliminate interpretation.

3. (T/F) When removing ambiguity, most translations take the same interpretive stance.

4. (T/F) Replacing the Bible's patriarchal language with inclusive language has no effect on the meaning of the text.

5. (T/F) English translations more often take away from the text than add to it.

6. Which of the following refers to the words that you do not use but do understand?
   a) Formal equivalence
   b) Dynamic equivalence
   c) Active vocabulary
   d) Passive vocabulary

7. Which of the following lends itself to a type of translation that can be much more interpretive?
   a) Formal equivalence
   b) Dynamic equivalence
   c) Active vocabulary
   d) Passive vocabulary

8. Which of the following focuses more on the structure of language than the connection of meaning?
   a) Formal equivalence
   b) Dynamic equivalence
   c) Active vocabulary
   d) Passive vocabulary

9. Age, Christian vocabulary, sentence complexity, and alliteration are all concerns of:
   a) Theology
   b) Ambiguity
   c) Exegesis
   d) Audience

10. We use _____ in translation when the Bible is more explicit than our culture.
    a) Euphemisms
    b) Interpretation
    c) Inclusive language
    d) Ambiguity

ANSWER KEY

1. T, 2. F, 3. T, 4. F, 5. F, 6. d, 7. b, 8. a, 9. d, 10. a

CHAPTER 33

How to Read a Commentary

You Should Know

- Exegesis: a fancy word for Bible study; drawing the meaning out of the text, learning what the author wanted to say
- Eisegesis: reading one's own meaning into the text
- Hermeneutics: the science and art of biblical interpretation
- The two steps of hermeneutics:
    i. Learn what the author meant to convey to his original audience.
    ii. Take what the passage meant and see what it means today.
- Grammatical-Historical Method: using grammar and an understanding of the book's historical setting as the primary tool of exegesis
- Allegorical method: an interpretive method that focuses on similarities and associations between a text and other texts, the spiritual life, history, or other facets
- Genre: a type of literature
- Setting: the historical, cultural, geographic, and theological background that informs a text
- Analogy of faith: a hermeneutical principle that came from the Reformation that asserts that the biblical authors do not contradict themselves
- The best exegesis begins with you and your Bible.

Essay Questions

1. What is the best way to begin exegesis? Why? What is the role of a commentary in exegesis?

2. What are the two phases of hermeneutics? Give an example of how they might be used in exegesis or ministry.

Quiz

1. (T/F) The best exegesis begins with you and a commentary.

2. (T/F) Eisegesis means reading your own meaning into the text.

3. (T/F) The number of footnotes is a good indicator of a commentary's quality.

4. (T/F) The first step of hermeneutics is to find out what the text means to us today.

5. (T/F) Commentators who use words like "clearly" and "obviously" are trustworthy.

6. History, culture, and geography all concern a text's:
   a) Genre
   b) Setting
   c) Theology
   d) None of the above

7. Which of the following terms refers to a type of literature?
   a) Commentary
   b) Hermeneutics
   c) Setting
   d) Genre

8. Which of the following asserts that the biblical authors do not contradict themselves?
   a) The Analogy of Faith
   b) The Grammatical-Historical Method

c) The allegorical method
d) Hermeneutics

9. What provides checks and balances against your possible interpretive mistakes?

   a) A commentary
   b) The allegorical method
   c) Exegesis
   d) The analogy of faith

10. What is the process by which we interpret, understand, and apply the Bible?

    a) Textus Receptus
    b) The allegorical method
    c) Hermeneutics
    d) Eisegesis

ANSWER KEY

1. F, 2. T, 3. F, 4. F, 5. F, 6. b, 7. d, 8. a, 9. a, 10. c

Notes

www.ingramcontent.com/pod-product-compliance
Lightning Source LLC
LaVergne TN
LVHW030634080426
835508LV00023B/3370